LOUISIANA

in words and pictures

BY DENNIS B. FRADIN

MAPS BY LEN W. MEENTS

Consultant:
   William V. Trufant
   President, Louisiana Historical Society
   New Orleans

 CHILDRENS PRESS, CHICAGO

For Nate Bossen

For their help, the author thanks:
William V. Trufant, President, Louisiana Historical Society
Louisiana State Library
Dave Davis, Assistant Professor, Anthropology Department,
Tulane University
Susan Bains, Oil and Gas Librarian, Railroad Commission of Texas

A Louisiana bayou

Library of Congress Cataloging in Publication Data

Fradin, Dennis B
    Louisiana in words and pictures.

    SUMMARY: Brief introduction to the history of
the Pelican State and its geography, industries,
cities, major tourist attractions, and famous
citizens.
    1. Louisiana—Juvenile literature. [1. Louisi-
ana] II. Meents, Len W. III. Title.
F369.3.F7   976.3   80-28609
ISBN 0-516-03918-0

Picture Acknowledgments:
BATON ROUGE AREA CONVENTION AND VISITORS BUREAU—Cover,
page 4, 11
JAMES P. ROWAN—pages 2, 12, 20 (top and bottom left and middle
right), 21 (left), 23
JUDITH BLOOM FRADIN—pages 6, 20 (top right), 21 (right), 22, 31, 40
STATE OF LOUISIANA OFFICE OF TOURISM—pages 7, 24, 25, 29, 30
(right), 33, 34, 35
JAY ELLEDGE, LAFAYETTE, LA—pages 9, 38
LAFAYETTE PARISH CONVENTION AND VISITORS COMMISSION,
LAFAYETTE, LA—pages 17, 30 (left), 42
DELTA QUEEN STEAMBOAT CO., CINCINNATI, OH—page 13
SMITHSONIAN INSTITUTION—page 15
DEPARTMENT OF THE ARMY, LOWER MISSISSIPPI VALLEY, CORPS
OF ENGINEERS—page 19
LOUISIANA STATE TOURIST DEVELOPMENT COMMISSION—pages
27, 28
BOB DENNIE, DEPARTMENT OF WILDLIFE AND FISHERIES, NEW
ORLEANS—page 37

COVER: The steamboat *Natchez*

Louisiana

Louisiana (loo • ee • zee • AN • ah) is in the far southern United States. It was named after Louis (LOO • ee) XIV. He was king of France in the 1600s.

Louisiana's nicknames tell you about the state. Many pelicans can be seen in Louisiana. These birds give Louisiana its main nickname, the *Pelican State.* Creoles (CREE • ohlz) are people of French and Spanish background. Many Creoles live in Louisiana. So Louisiana is sometimes called the *Creole State.* Sugarcane is grown in the state. So Louisiana is called the *Sugar State.* It is also called the *Bayou* (BYE • yoo) *State.* That nickname comes from the bayous found near the Mississippi River. Bayous are slow-moving waters.

Do you know which state is first in producing natural gas? Or which is second in producing oil? Or where pirate Jean Laffite (ZHAHN lah • FEET) helped the United States win a big battle? Do you know where jazz music was born? Or where the world's longest bridge is located? You will soon see that the answer to all these questions is: Louisiana!

Today, some of Louisiana is covered by swamps and bayous. But millions of years ago all of Louisiana was under water. How do scientists know this? Because fossils of sea animals have been found in many places that are now dry land. In 1980 the remains of a whale were found in central Louisiana.

A swamp in the Baton Rouge area

People first came to Louisiana at least 12,000 years ago. These first people roamed the area to hunt. They killed deer, saber-toothed cats, and other animals. Stone spearpoints and tools of the early people have been found.

Much more recently, as many as thirty Indian tribes lived in Louisiana. Some of the tribes were:

The Chitimacha (chihd • uh • MAH • sha)

The Attakapa (at • ah • KAH • pah)

The Houma (HOW • mah)

The Choctaw (CHAHK • taw)

The Acolapissa (ah • kuh • lah • PIH • suh)

The Caddo (KAH • doh)

Modern Indians farmed. Corn and beans were two of their main crops. Indians who farmed could stay in one place. They built houses of wood, leaves, and mud. Many houses formed a village.

The Lafitte Cemetery shown here is at the site of a Choctaw burial mound

The Indians also hunted deer, bears, and other animals. They fished. Near the coast, the Indians gathered clams.

Spanish explorers were the first non-Indians in Louisiana. Spaniard Hernando De Soto (her • NAN • doh deh SO • toe) arrived in 1541. He was on a long trip in search of gold. De Soto didn't find gold. He died in 1542. He was buried in the Mississippi River.

In 1682 French explorer La Salle arrived. He took a canoe trip down the Mississippi River. On April 9, 1682, La Salle reached what is now southeast Louisiana. He found the place where the Mississippi River empties into the Gulf of Mexico. There, La Salle placed a cross in the mud. He claimed a huge area for France. He named it *Louisiana* for his king.

For more than 100 years, France and then Spain and then France again controlled Louisiana.

The first period of French rule was between 1699 and 1762. During this time some Frenchmen came to trade with the Indians for furs. The French also built Louisiana's first towns. Natchitoches (NAHK • ih • tawsh) was the very first non-Indian town built in what is now Louisiana. It was founded in 1714 by Louis Juchereau de St. Denis (LOO • ee yoo • care • OH duh sahn deh • NEES). It was a trading post and a fort.

These two buildings still stand in Natchitoches, the oldest town in the Louisiana Purchase territory. Roque House (below) was built in 1803. Lemee House (left) was built in 1830.

In 1718 a French Canadian began building New Orleans (noo OHR • lenz). He had a long name: Jean Baptiste le Moyne, Sieur de Bienville (ZHAHN bap • TEEST leh MWANH, syure deh byanh • VEEL). In its early years New Orleans was damaged by hurricanes. But by 1721 the town had 400 people. And it was growing. It became the most important town in Louisiana—as it is today.

The French saw that Louisiana had good farmland. Large farms were built in southern Louisiana. They were called *plantations*. The French brought in black slaves. They did the work on the plantations. Cotton and sugarcane were grown. So was indigo. Indigo is a plant used to dye clothes blue.

In 1762 Spain gained control of Louisiana. Spanish people arrived. Some of them set up plantations, too.

Restored buildings at Acadian Village in Lafayette

There are people in Louisiana today who are the great-great-great grandchildren of the early settlers. The descendants of the early French and Spanish settlers are called *Creoles*. From the 1760s to 1790 some French people came from Canada. They were called *Acadians* (ah • KADE • ee • unz). Their descendants are called *Cajuns* (KAY • junz).

In 1800 Spain returned Louisiana to France. But this time the French controlled it for just a short time.

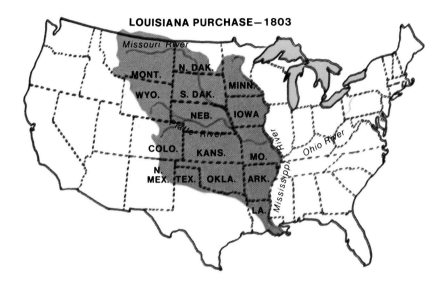

LOUISIANA PURCHASE—1803

A new country had been formed in 1776. This was the United States of America. In 1803 the young United States bought a large piece of land from France. The United States paid France $15 million. This may sound like a lot of money. But the United States received a *very* big piece of land. It was so big that 15 states were later made from it. What is now the state of Louisiana was just part of that piece of land. The land deal was called the *Louisiana Purchase* (PURR • chuss).

Americans now poured in. Many came from nearby southern states. By 1810 Louisiana had more than 75,000 people. "Make Louisiana a state!" people said.

The old state capitol (left) looks like a medieval castle. Above: A view of the old state capitol dome

On April 30, 1812, Louisiana became our eighteenth state. New Orleans was the first state capital. Many years later Baton Rouge (bat • en ROOZH) became the capital. It still is today.

Soon after Louisiana became a state the War of 1812 began. In this war the United States and England fought about trade and shipping. The last battle of this war was fought in Louisiana.

In late 1814 about 8,000 English soldiers marched toward New Orleans. They wanted to capture the city. United States forces were led by Andrew Jackson. He later became president. Jackson used soldiers, Indians, slaves, and free black people to defend New Orleans. The famous pirate Jean Laffite and his fellow pirates also helped the Americans win the Battle of New Orleans. It was fought on January 8, 1815.

In the early 1800s thousands of people came to Louisiana to farm. Many built small farms. They grew corn and other crops. On these farms, the people had to work hard just to produce enough food for themselves.

Some people built sugar and cotton plantations. The plantation owners lived like kings and queens. They hunted foxes and even alligators. They dressed up for dances and parties.

This blacksmith shop in New Orleans (below) was used by pirate Jean Lafitte as a front for smuggled goods.

A few steamboats, including the *Delta Queen* (above), still travel on the Mississippi River.

The wealth of the planters depended on cotton and sugar. Getting the crops to market was hard. Often they were sent on boats that had oars. Then a new kind of boat—the steamboat—was invented. Its power came from an engine. In 1812 the steamboat *New Orleans* came down the Mississippi River. It was the first steamboat to do this. After that, steamboats were used to carry cotton to New Orleans. There the cotton was bought by cotton merchants. It was sent to mills outside Louisiana. Then it was made into clothes. Cotton became such an important crop that it was called "King Cotton."

You remember that the planters used slaves to grow their crops. In the 1850s Northerners and Southerners argued about slavery. There was talk that United States lawmakers would end slavery. This angered many Southerners. Southerners were also upset about taxes, called *tariffs* (TARE • iffs). They had to pay tariffs on goods bought from Europe. Southerners spoke of "States' Rights." They felt that each state should decide for itself about tariffs, slavery, and other issues.

Finally, Southern states left the United States. Southerners formed their own country. It was called the Confederate (kun • FED • uh • rut) States of America.

War between the Confederate (Southern) and Union (Northern) states began in 1861. This was the start of the Civil War. Louisiana joined the Confederacy. Louisiana sent about 65,000 men to the Confederate army.

Commander David Farragut's fleet in combat on the
Mississippi River during the Civil War

There were no huge Civil War battles in Louisiana.
But in 1862 the war did come to the state. David
Farragut (FAIR • uh • gut) led some Union gunboats up
the Mississippi River. The ships attacked the forts that
guarded New Orleans. The Union Army then took over
New Orleans. Farragut also helped the Union take
control of Baton Rouge. As the Union Army entered
Louisiana, there was much destruction.

The South had fewer soldiers than the North. It had
fewer supplies. In 1865 the Confederacy lost the Civil
War.

In 1868 Louisiana was once again part of the United
States. But the state was in ruins. United States soldiers

stayed in Louisiana to maintain order and support the elected officials. Most of these officials were Northerners and freed slaves. The Northerners who came to the South were called *carpetbaggers*. This was because many of them carried their belongings to the South in carpetbags. These were suitcases made from carpeting.

This was a sad time in Louisiana history. Blacks and whites fought each other. Northerners and Southerners disliked each other. It almost seemed as if the Civil War were still being fought. In 1877, soldiers were finally sent out of Louisiana. Louisiana people then began the job of rebuilding their state.

The slaves had been freed. This meant that the plantation system was finished. Some black people and white people became sharecroppers. They farmed land owned by others. They had to share their crops with the landowners. Some people became tenant farmers. They kept their own crops. But they had to pay rent for the land. Sharecroppers and tenant farmers were often very poor. But all these farmers helped Louisiana become an important farm state once more.

You remember that De Soto once came to Louisiana in search of gold. He did not find it. But in the 1900s treasures *were* found in the state's ground. Not gold, but oil, was found in 1901. It was later found in many places in Louisiana. Today, Louisiana is the second leading oil-producing state. Our country needs oil to run cars and machines.

In 1916 natural gas was found in Louisiana. By 1979 Louisiana was the top state in the production of natural gas. The gas is needed to heat houses and cook food. Louisiana is also a top state for mining salt.

This offshore oil rig in the Gulf of Mexico is right off the Louisiana coast.

Manufacturing (making things in factories) has also become very big in the 1900s. Chemicals are made in Louisiana. Oil and coal products are also made there. Foods are packaged in Louisiana factories.

You have learned about some of Louisiana's history. Now it is time for a trip—in words and pictures— through the Pelican State.

Louisiana is shaped much like an old boot. Yes, it looks like an "old" boot. The islands and lakes in the southeast make the boot look torn around the toes! Arkansas (AR • kun • saw) is Louisiana's neighbor state to the north. Mississippi is to the east. The Gulf of Mexico (MEKS • ih • koh) is the big body of water to the south and southeast. Texas (TEKS • us) is the state to the west.

Pretend you're in an airplane high above Louisiana. From there you can see how flat the land is. The flat lands that make up Louisiana are called *plains*. Louisiana's plains make it one of our flattest states.

New Orleans from the air, just as you would see it from a plane

From the air you can also see many lakes, marshes, and swamps. Pretend you can see that huge river that flows down Louisiana's eastern side. That is our country's main river—the Mississippi River.

Your airplane is landing in a big city on the Mississippi River. This is New Orleans. It is in southeast Louisiana. Once, Choctaw and other Indians lived here. The Sieur de Bienville founded New Orleans in 1718. The city was named for a French nobleman, the Duke of Orleans. Today, New Orleans is by far Louisiana's biggest city. About a third of all Louisiana people live in the New Orleans area.

The French Quarter, shown in these pictures, is the oldest part of New Orleans. The St. Louis Cathedral is shown in the top left picture. The Presbytere (middle right) was once a courthouse. It is now a museum. Notice the fancy ironwork balconies in the picture at the top of the page on the right.

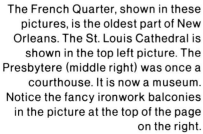

Above: Artists line Jackson Square in the French
Quarter.
Left: Brennan's, one of the many excellent
restaurants in the French Quarter

Visit the city's famous French Quarter. This is the oldest part of New Orleans. Some buildings there are more than 150 years old. They are in both French and Spanish styles. French Quarter buildings are known for the fancy ironwork on the balconies. You will enjoy the house called Madame John's Legacy (LEG • uh • see). It was built by a French sea captain back in the 1720s. The St. Louis Cathedral (SAYNT LOO • iss kuh • THEE • drull) in the French Quarter was built in 1794. It is the oldest Catholic cathedral still in use in the United States.

Do you like food better than old buildings? French Quarter restaurants are world-famous for their tasty Creole food.

A new kind of music became popular in New Orleans in the early 1900s. People called it *jazz*. Many of the first jazz musicians were black. Some think that jazz was born at funerals! On the way to a funeral, the musicians played sad music. But on the way back, they played "hot," lively tunes. Because jazz began there, New Orleans became known as the "Cradle of Jazz." Preservation Hall in the French Quarter is just one place where you can hear jazz music in New Orleans today.

You don't have to go to Preservation Hall to hear jazz in New Orleans. This jazz band is playing outdoors in Jackson Square.

Above: A stately mansion in the Garden District
Left: A beautiful New Orleans courtyard

There is a lot more to New Orleans than the French Quarter. One area is known as the Garden District. After the United States bought Louisiana in 1803, rich Americans moved into this area. Confederate president Jefferson Davis died at a house in the Garden District. You can see huge old houses built by cotton merchants and other wealthy people in many places in New Orleans. Long Vue Gardens is one of the prettiest.

The people of New Orleans work at many jobs. Some package foods. Others make ships. There is a rocket factory in New Orleans. A rocket that helped send our first astronauts to the moon was made there.

A ship docked at the Port of New Orleans

New Orleans is one of our country's main port cities. Ships at the Port of New Orleans take products in and out of our country.

New Orleans has many fine museums. At the Louisiana State Museum you can learn about Louisiana history. New Orleans is also home to many fine colleges. The University of New Orleans and Tulane (too • LAYNE) University are just two of them.

New Orleans has one of the best-known celebrations in the United States. It is called Mardi Gras (MAR • dee grah). It is held in February or March, before the Catholic period called Lent begins. For about two weeks

Above and left: Mardi Gras scenes
Right: The Louisiana Superdome,
where the Sugar Bowl
football game is played

there are parades and fancy parties known as "balls." On Mardi Gras Day, almost the whole city comes out for a party in the streets! People wear masks and costumes. Bands play. About a million people from all over the world come each year to Mardi Gras.

You can also enjoy sports in New Orleans. The Saints are the city's football team. They play in a large stadium called the Louisiana Superdome. Each New Year's Day a famous college football game is played in the Superdome. It is called the Sugar Bowl game.

There is one more fact you might like to know about New Orleans. It has the world's longest bridge. It is 29 miles long. The bridge is called the Lake Pontchartrain Causeway (PAHN • chur • trayne CAWS • way). It connects New Orleans to its suburbs in the north.

After seeing New Orleans, head northwest. Go along the Mississippi River to Baton Rouge. Once, Bayou Goula (BYE • yoo GOO • lah) and Houma Indians lived here. According to a story, a big red stick divided the lands of the two tribes. Frenchmen built a fort here in 1719. They named it *Baton Rouge* (meaning "red stick" in French). Today, Baton Rouge is the second biggest city in Louisiana. It is also the capital of the state.

Visit the state capitol building. Of all 50 state capitol buildings in our country, this is the tallest. It is 34 stories high.

Walk up the 49 steps to the entrance. The names of the 50 states are engraved on the steps. The names of the last two states—Alaska and Hawaii—are both on the top step.

Inside the state capitol you can watch lawmakers working on laws for Louisiana. The governor also has his office in the building. One famous Louisiana governor was Huey Long. Long was shot to death in this building in 1935. Huey Long is buried on the capitol grounds. There is also a statue of him on the grounds.

The old state capitol is also in Baton Rouge. It was built in 1847.

The new state capitol in Baton Rouge (below) was completed in 1932.

Rosedown Plantation and Gardens in St. Francisville

Baton Rouge is home to Louisiana State University. Students there study to be teachers and lawyers. They also study music, business, and many other subjects. Southern University is also in Baton Rouge.

Continue up the Mississippi River from Baton Rouge. You will come to the town of St. Francisville (SAYNT FRAN • siss • vihl). You can see plantations in and near St. Francisville. Parlange (pahr • LANZH) Plantation and Rosedown Plantation and Gardens are just two of them. You will enjoy Oakley Plantation. The famous artist

Rich farmland along the Mississippi River

John James Audubon did some pictures for his book
Birds of America here.

The Mississippi River brings rich soil down to its
mouth in Louisiana. The soil deposited here over
hundreds of years has formed a *delta*. Delta soil is among
the best in the world. That is one reason why you will see
many farms along the Mississippi River. Louisiana gets a
lot of rain. It also has a long growing season because it is
so far south. Good soil, rainfall, and warm weather make
the delta—and most of Louisiana—great for farming.

You would have a good diet if you ate nothing but Louisiana farm products! A lot of soybeans are grown along the delta. They are Louisiana's main crop. In the southern part of the state you will see lots of sugarcane and rice. Louisiana is a leading state for growing both those crops. Corn, sweet potatoes (known as *Louisiana yams*), and many kinds of fruits and vegetables are grown in the state. There is one important Louisiana crop you can't eat. But you might have clothes made from it. This is cotton. You will also see cattle in Louisiana. The cattle on ranches are raised for beef. On dairy farms, the cows give milk. Chickens and hogs are raised in the state, too.

Below: A farmer harvests sugarcane, one of Louisiana's main crops.
Right: Cattle on a Louisiana ranch

Look at a map. You will see that the Mississippi River forms the border along the northeastern part of the state. Follow the Mississippi River northward. Today, you will see barges and ships on the river. More than 100 years ago you would have seen steamboats. Steamboats sometimes had races. In 1870, the *Robert E. Lee* and the *Natchez* (NACH • ehz) raced from New Orleans to St. Louis. The *Lee* won with a time of 3 days, 18 hours, and 14 minutes. You can still take steamboat rides on the Mississippi River for fun.

The Mississippi River has flooded many times. You will see walls called *levees* along the river. The levees help keep towns and farms from flooding.

The steamboat *Natchez* at the Port of New Orleans (below) takes visitors on Mississippi River cruises.

Near Louisiana's northeast corner you will come to a group of dirt mounds. They are called the Poverty Point Indian Mounds. They were built by Indians 3,000 years ago. Many stone tools and ancient artworks have been found at the mounds. One of the mounds there is shaped like a huge bird.

Monroe (mun • ROE) is the largest city in northeast Louisiana. Think of Monroe the next time you see car headlights at night. Headlights, chemicals, and furniture are just three of the products made in the Monroe area.

About 100 miles west of Monroe you will come to Shreveport (SHREEV • port). Shreveport lies in northwest Louisiana, on the Red River. Caddo Indians once hunted and fished here. The first settlers arrived in 1834. The town that grew up here was named Shreveport, for Henry Shreve. He opened northwest Louisiana to settlement. The story of how he did it is one of the most interesting in Louisiana's history.

Statue of Henry Shreve, who cleared much of the Red River

Back in the 1800s, a main way of traveling was by boat. But there was a problem in northwest Louisiana at that time. The Red River was blocked by a huge log jam. This jam was many miles long. People said it would never be cleared. But Henry Shreve invented what he called "snag boats." With them he bulldozed the logs out of the way. By about 1838 Shreve had cleared much of the river. This helped the growth of Shreveport and other towns in northwest Louisiana.

Today, Shreveport is the third biggest city in Louisiana. It is an important manufacturing city. Metal and wood products are made there.

Visit the State Fairgrounds in Shreveport. Every October, the Louisiana State Fair is held there.

You will see oil wells near Shreveport—and in many areas of the state. Only Texas produces more oil than Louisiana. Louisiana is the leading state in the production of natural gas.

Natchitoches is southeast of Shreveport. You remember that Natchitoches is Louisiana's oldest town. You will enjoy seeing the old houses there.

Kisatchie National Forest is near Natchitoches. In all, about half of Louisiana is wooded. Pines, oaks, and maples are three kinds of trees you will see in Louisiana forests. Some trees are cut down. Paper and lumber are just two of Louisiana's forest products.

Kisatchie
National Forest

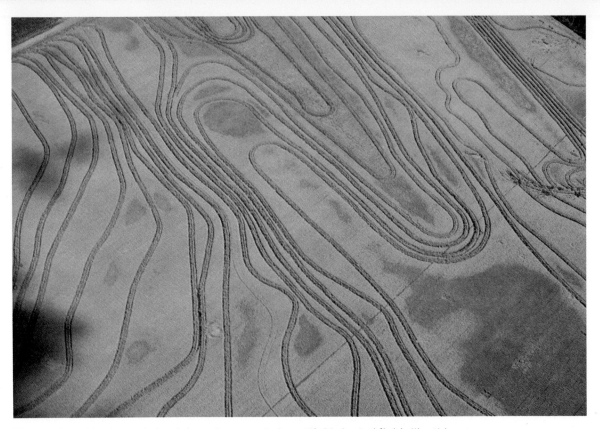
Rice, an important crop in Louisiana, is grown in beautiful irrigated fields like this one.

Go near Louisiana's southwest corner. You will come to the city of Lake Charles. It lies on the Calcasieu (KAL • kuh • shoo) River, near some large lakes. A lot of rice is grown near Lake Charles. Rice is sent from Lake Charles to many places in the world. Oil products and chemicals are made in Lake Charles.

When you leave Lake Charles, head south. You will come to the Gulf of Mexico. The land along the water is known as the *Gulf Coast.*

35

Long ago, pirate ships sailed along the coast. Pirate Jean Laffite made his headquarters on Grand Isle. Many swamps and bayous of southern Louisiana are said to hide pirate treasure.

Today, a treasure is taken right from under the waters of the Gulf of Mexico. This modern-day treasure is oil.

You will see fishing boats going out into the Gulf of Mexico. Louisiana fishermen bring back tons of shrimp. They also bring back oysters, crabs, and menhaden (men • HAY • den).

You will also see interesting wildlife in southern Louisiana. You can spot foxes, bobcats, swamp rabbits, and bears. Alligators live in the marshes and bayous. You can find deer throughout the state.

Long ago, the fur trade was big business in America. It died out in most places. But fur trapping is still done in southern Louisiana. Muskrats are trapped. Nutrias (NOO • tree • uhz) are trapped, too. The furs of these animals are used to make coats.

Louisiana wildlife includes
brown pelicans (left), rabbits
(above), alligators (top right),
and snowy egrets (right).

Many birds can be seen along the Gulf Coast. Ducks
and geese spend their winter vacations in this warm
area. Brown pelicans—the state bird—catch fish in the
marshes. Snowy egrets (EE • gretz) can be seen. Snowy
egrets were once hunted for their feathers. They were
nearly wiped out. E.A. McIlhenny (MACK • ill • hen • ee),
who lived on Avery Island, went through the swamps
and found a few egrets. He protected them, and the
number of snowy egrets grew.

These shrimp boats are taking part in the annual Shrimp Festival in Delacambre, just south of Lafayette. During the festival, the "blessing of the fleet" ceremony takes place. The fishermen feel that this will help them have a good season.

It is time to finish your Louisiana trip. Go north of Avery Island to the city of Lafayette (lah • fee • YET). It is famous for its lovely gardens and flower shows.

The Lafayette area is sometimes called *Cajun Country.* Many Cajun people live in Lafayette and in the nearby towns. Some Cajuns still speak French in their daily life—just as the first Louisiana settlers did long ago.

Places can't tell the whole story of Louisiana. Many interesting people have lived in the state.

Pierre (PYAIR) G.T. Beauregard (BOH • reh • gard) (1818-1893) was born near New Orleans. During the Civil War Beauregard was a Confederate general. He gave the order for the Confederates to fire on Fort Sumter. Those were the first shots of the Civil War. Beauregard led Southern soldiers in other important battles.

Huey Long (1893-1935) was born near Winnfield, Louisiana. He served as governor of Louisiana from 1928 to 1932. Later, he became a United States senator. He had so much power that people called him the "Kingfish." Huey Long planned to run for president. But he was shot to death in 1935.

Lillian Hellman was born in New Orleans in 1905. She became a famous writer. Lillian Hellman wrote plays.

Street entertainers perform in the streets of New Orleans today, just as Louis Armstrong did so long ago.

The Little Foxes and *Watch on the Rhine* are just two of them.

Louis (LOO • ee) Armstrong (1900-1971) was born in New Orleans on the Fourth of July. As a child he loved music—especially jazz. He formed a group that sang for coins on the streets of New Orleans. Later Louis Armstrong became a famous jazz musician. He played the trumpet. He sang. The great "Satchmo" also appeared in movies. Buddy Bolden and Jelly Roll Morton were just two other jazz musicians born in New Orleans.

Mahalia (mah • HALE • yah) Jackson (1911-1972) was born in New Orleans, too. She became a famous gospel singer. That means she sang religious (ree • LIH • jus) songs. Mahalia Jackson was a black woman. She felt that her music helped bring black people and white people closer together.

Andrew Young was born in New Orleans in 1932. He became a civil rights leader. Then he became a Georgia lawmaker. Did you ever hear of the United Nations? It is a group that works to keep world peace. In 1977 Andrew Young became the first black person to serve as our country's United Nations ambassador.

Michael DeBakey (MIKE • ull deh • BAKE • ee) was born in Lake Charles, Louisiana in 1908. As a boy, he liked science. DeBakey became a surgeon (SIR • jun). He found new ways to help people with bad hearts. Dr. DeBakey has helped save thousands of people with heart trouble.

Bill Russell was born in Monroe, Louisiana in 1934. He became a great pro basketball player. Russell helped the Boston Celtics (SELL • ticks) win 11 NBA championships.

Wild iris along a Louisiana bayou

He also coached the Celtics. Bill Russell was the first black person to coach a major pro sports team. Basketball star Elvin Hayes, football quarterback Terry Bradshaw, and baseball pitcher Vida Blue (VYE • dah BLOO) are three other athletes from Louisiana.

Birthplace of Huey Long . . . Lillian Hellman . . . Louis Armstrong . . . and jazz music.

The land of bayous . . . swamps . . . the Gulf Coast . . . and the Mississippi River delta.

A state where you can see old plantations and new factories.

Now a leader for producing oil . . . natural gas . . . rice . . . and sugarcane.

This is the Pelican State—Louisiana!

Facts About LOUISIANA

Area—48,523 square miles (31st biggest state)

Greatest Distance North to South—237 miles

Greatest Distance East to West—236½ miles

Borders—Arkansas to the north; Mississippi to the east; the Gulf of Mexico to the south and southeast; Texas to the west

Highest Point—535 feet above sea level (Driskill Mountain)

Lowest Point—Five feet below sea level (in New Orleans)

Hottest Recorded Temperature—114°F. (at Plain Dealing, on August 10, 1936)

Coldest Recorded Temperature—Minus 16°F. (at Minden, on February 13, 1899)

Statehood—Our 18th state, on April 30, 1812

Origin of Name—The French explorer La Salle named Louisiana for Louis XIV, king of France

Capital—Baton Rouge

Parishes (called counties in other states)—64

U.S. Senators—2

U.S. Representatives—8

State Senators—39

State Representatatives—105

State Song—"Give Me Louisiana," by Doralice Fontane

State Motto—*Union, Justice, and Confidence*

Main Nickname—The Pelican State

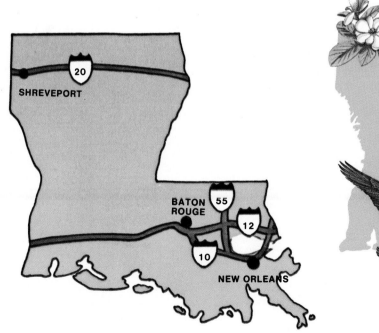

43

Other Nicknames—The Bayou State, the Creole State, the Sugar State,
   Sportsman's Paradise
State Seal—Adopted in 1902
State Flag—Adopted in 1912
State Flower—Magnolia
State Bird—Brown pelican
State Insect—Honeybee
State Tree—Bald cypress
State Fossil—Petrified palmwood
State Gemstone—Agate
State Colors—Gold, white, and blue
Main River—Mississippi River
Some Other Rivers—Red, Atchafalaya, Pearl, Calcasieu, Sabine, Ouachita
Largest Lake—Lake Pontchartrain
Wildlife—Deer, bobcats, bears, rabbits, muskrats, minks, raccoons, opossums,
   skunks, otters, squirrels, weasels, foxes, beavers, nutrias, alligators,
   snapping turtles and other turtles, water moccasins and other snakes,
   ducks, geese, pelicans, snowy egrets, many other kinds of birds
Fishing—Menhaden, shrimp, oysters, crabs
Farm Products—Soybeans, sugarcane, rice, cotton, sweet potatoes,
   strawberries, peaches, pecans, tobacco, beef cattle, milk, hogs, broiler
   chickens, eggs
Mining—Oil, natural gas, salt, sulfur, lignite
Manufacturing Products—Chemicals, oil and coal products, packaged foods,
   wood products, plastics, clothes, metal products
Population—3,921,000 (1977 estimate)
Major Cities—New Orleans   555,000 (1979 estimates)
              Baton Rouge   213,000
              Shreveport   189,000
              Metairie   172,200
              Lafayette   79,900
              Lake Charles   75,700

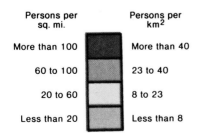

Persons per sq. mi.		Persons per km²
More than 100		More than 40
60 to 100		23 to 40
20 to 60		8 to 23
Less than 20		Less than 8

44

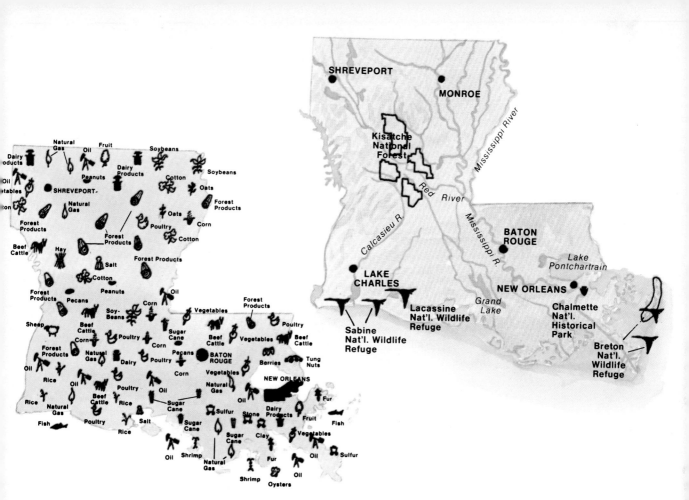

Louisiana History

There were people in Louisiana at least 12,000 years ago.

1541—Spanish explorer De Soto enters Louisiana while searching for gold

1682—French explorer La Salle comes by canoe down the Mississippi River;
he claims a large area for France and names it Louisiana to honor his
king

1699—Louisiana becomes a French colony

1714—Natchitoches, now Louisiana's oldest town, is founded

1718—New Orleans is founded by Bienville, a French-Canadian explorer

1719—Baton Rouge is founded by French soldiers

1762—Control of Louisiana passes from France to Spain

Late 1760s—French people called *Acadians* begin to arrive from Canada;
their descendants are called *Cajuns*

1794—Louisiana's first newspaper *Le Moniteur de la Louisiane* (the *Louisiana
Monitor*) is printed in French at New Orleans

1800—Spain returns Louisiana to France

1803—By the Louisiana Purchase, the United States buys much land from
France, including what is now Louisiana

1812—On April 30, Louisiana becomes our 18th state; New Orleans is the capital

1815—In the Battle of New Orleans (the last battle of the War of 1812) Andrew Jackson's forces beat the English

1830—Population of Louisiana is 215,739

1834—Shreveport area is settled

1838—First Mardi Gras parade is held in New Orleans

1853—Yellow fever plague hits state and kills 11,000 in New Orleans alone

1861—Louisiana leaves the United States and joins the Confederacy; Louisiana sends about 65,000 men to fight in the Confederate (Southern) Army

1862—New Orleans and Baton Rouge are captured by Union forces

1865—Union wins Civil War; Louisiana and other Southern states are in ruins

1868—Louisiana once again becomes part of the United States

1877—U.S. troops finally leave Louisiana

1882—Baton Rouge becomes Louisiana's permanent capital

1900—Population of Louisiana is 1,381,625

1901—Oil is found in Louisiana

1916—Natural gas is found

1917-1918—After the United States enters World War I, Louisiana provides more than 74,000 soldiers for the armed forces

1928—Huey P. Long becomes governor of the state

1932—New state capitol building is completed in Baton Rouge

1935—Huey Long is shot to death

1941-1945—After the United States enters World War II, 260,000 Louisiana men and women are in uniform

1950—Population of the Pelican State reaches 2,683,516

1956—The Lake Ponchartrain Causeway—the world's longest bridge—opens

1957—Hurricane Audrey kills hundreds in Louisiana, Mississippi, and Texas

1963—A canal called the Mississippi River-Gulf Outlet is opened to boat traffic; it provides a shortcut from New Orleans to the Gulf of Mexico

1969—Hurricane Camille kills more than 250 people and causes great destruction in a seven-state area that includes Louisiana

1973—Corrine Morrison Boggs is the first woman ever elected to the U.S. Congress from Louisiana

1975—Present state constitution goes into effect; in this same year the Louisiana Superdome opens in New Orleans

1977—Ernest N. Morial is elected mayor of New Orleans; he becomes the first black person to serve as mayor of the city

1980—David C. Treen becomes governor

INDEX

INDEX, Cont'd.

About the Author:

Dennis Fradin attended Northwestern University on a creative writing scholarship and graduated in 1967. While still at Northwestern, he published his first stories in *Ingenue* magazine and also won a prize in *Seventeen's* short story competition. A prolific writer, Dennis Fradin has been regularly publishing stories in such diverse places as *The Saturday Evening Post, Scholastic, National Humane Review, Midwest,* and *The Teaching Paper.* He has also scripted several educational films. Since 1970 he has taught second grade reading in a Chicago school—a rewarding job, which, the author says, "provides a captive audience on whom I test my children's stories." Married and the father of three children, Dennis Fradin spends his free time with his family or playing a myriad of sports and games with his childhood chums.

About the Artist:

Len Meents studied painting and drawing at Southern Illinois University and after graduation in 1969 he moved to Chicago. Mr. Meents works full time as a painter and illustrator. He and his wife and child currently make their home in LaGrange, Illinois.